Taking Back Your Holidays

A Whimsical Guide to a Lighter, Brighter Christmas

Yvonne Lacey

Dr. Xmas®
… with your prescription for the holidays!

Publishing Services provided by Paper Raven Books

Printed in the United States of America

First Printing, 2017

Paperback ISBN= 978-0-9994643-0-4
Hardback ISBN= 978-0-9994643-1-1

I grew up in a household where Christmas was fraught with statements from my mother, like (when my dad presented her with a mink stole), "Maybe next year, you can get the rest of the coat."

So, needless to say, I never imagined I'd come to appreciate the holiday season.

And then I met Yvonne Lacey.

Picture it: Los Angeles, in the early days of the 21st century. Yvonne and I had begun working together at a major broadcast TV network. And from the moment we met, I knew she had the potential to turn my fear of Christmas around. You see, Yvonne exudes joy and kindness, and her love for the holiday season is well known and unbounded.

And over the years, she has indeed turned me round, right round, like a record, baby, right round, and I now share her irresistible delight in the holiday season. She has, in fact, become an ambassador for Christmas. As Dr. Xmas, she is our digital Santa's Helper, who hosts both a wildly popular blog and podcast.

As her Dr. Xmas fame grew, many of us pressed her to write a book—and what a book she has delivered. Filled with practical tips and humorous history, it'll remind you of why we go through these insane weeks each year, and show you how to truly enjoy the holidays and not just muddle through them.

So, tell your inner kid it's safe to come out. Then, grab a candy cane or hot cocoa, slip on a cozy sweater, and let Dr. Xmas remind you that there is indeed magic in them thar holiday moments.

~ Eric Poole
Author of *Where's My Wand: One Boy's Magical Triumph Over Alienation and Shag Carpeting* and *Excuse Me While I Slip Into Someone More Comfortable* (5/15/18)

For my mother, whose joy for Christmas, and her children, knew no bounds …

Miss you, mom!

"Love is the stuff that's left in the room after all the Christmas presents are unwrapped."

~ Anonymous 5-year old

INTRODUCTION

Taking Back Your Holidays

In a world where we are often so busy that we forget what day of the week it is, and find it hard to believe that a whole season has already flown by, it's time to take back our moments.

How do we do this? Since there is no real way to stop time from moving forward (at least we haven't quite figured it out yet and, currently, there's no app for that), we must learn to give ourselves momentary time outs. And guess what! We already have that built into the calendar, folks. They're called holidays. All we have to do is honor them.

For almost every month in our annual calendar, we have a holiday. While some are more elaborate than others, they are all designed as respites from the challenges of our daily routines.

They are built in to take time out, to honor others, and to reflect on family and friends. But instead, what do we do? We make them into work. We plan, we arrange, we cram all we can into what we call long weekends. We overload and overdo and end up underwhelmed and usually more tired than rested. Good thing we had a holiday to begin with, right?

More than any of the other holidays (and those don't lag far behind), the Christmas holiday season becomes more challenging each year and, quite frankly, a chore to the point of exhaustion. For some, it's downright dreaded. So many traditions, so little time.

Even one of the most famous curmudgeons snarled it best, warning his nephew to "… keep Christmas in your own way and let me keep it in mine." And though Scrooge was mocking the very essence and joy of the holiday, he was right in urging us all to celebrate it in the best way we know how. That's the secret! But that's also the challenge.

Let me show you how to take back your holidays. Along the way, let's share the wonder of the season: silly, fun traditions, "who knew" insights into the origins and meanings of holiday rituals, and occasional deep and poignant thoughts about this wonderful time of year. Join me on my journey, and partake of the joy. Because, after all, that is what this magical season is all about.

~ Dr. Xmas

"Who is Dr. Xmas?"

Many years ago, when I was barely a gleam in my mother's eye, Christmas was in full swing at our house. From the dangling red ornaments to the shiny tinsel and brightly wrapped packages under that very hip tree, (can you say Mad Men era?) I was destined to join the party. And shortly thereafter, I did arrive to meet my brother and sister on a very special day, none other than December 25th. So, with that auspicious birth date, a love for holidays, and a zest for knowledge, I give you "Dr. Xmas."

"… and why do I need a doctor?"

"It's Christmastime again!" For some of you, those are frightening words. Holiday office parties, gift buying frenzies, crowded malls with long lines and traffic nightmares. Who needs it? Well, I think we all do. But we need the right prescription to cure the holiday ills. No, not the one in the medicine cabinet. This one's holistic.

True enough, the seasonal chores can create a tumultuous, if not downright traumatic, ripple effect. But the benefits far outweigh the costs. Let me remind you of hot cocoa, the lovely dancing flame of a burning candle, the familiar sweet smells from the kitchen, colorfully bright lights, carefully wrapped packages, visions of sugarplums, friends and family, miracles and small blessings alike, and a general all-around good feeling in the air. Akin to a warm cup of tomato soup on a cold wintry day, thoughts of Santa visiting once again in his red suit warm the hearts of both children and adults. This is what makes Christmas worthwhile.

So, maybe this year, do a little less "Christmas chore" and give a lot more Christmas cheer—you'll receive tenfold. Give a gift from the heart instead of shopping at the mall, by making a gift instead of buying one. Make a snow angel and decorate a cookie. Create your own miracle by doing something nice for someone else anonymously. Remember what it was like to be a child on Christmas morn, and hold on to that joy throughout the festivities.

Here's hoping that you will take on this season with vigor and use it as a sense of renewal and eternal hope. And, most important of all, have fun by making it your own! No one likes a Scrooge, and even he got the message in the end.

Make merry, be merry…

Table Of Contents

1

The Christmas Police

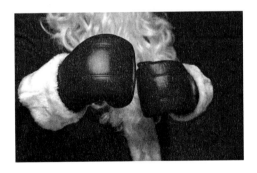

Y ou may have picked up this book because you are the ultimate Christmas fan, or maybe the very thought of Christmas makes you cringe. Even for those who are fans, let's admit it, there's a part of you that enters the holidays with a bit of trepidation. Christmas can bring out a whole range of yuletide sentiments, but no matter where you fall on that spectrum, I wrote this for YOU! Because, we could all use at least a little help making the most of the holiday season.

As much as I love the holidays and am excited about their arrival, I understand the cries of "Oh no, not again!" or even, "I hate this time of year!" With so much to do, in so little time, it's no wonder that we've become a little Grinch-y about the whole affair. So many reasons exist for bah-humbugging the entire holiday season: stress, commercialism, and a stream of holiday bills in January (not the best way to start the new year off or honor your savings plan resolution.) These can be justification enough to boycott Christmas altogether and head south for the winter.

After all, there's so much to do! There's not nearly enough time for Christmas shopping, planning the holiday meal, and wrapping presents (even at elf-gone-mad speeds). I can hear the voices of friends and family now as they run through their lists, working up a frenzy as they speak ...

"I'll need a new outfit for the annual Christmas party and a haircut. Need to do that soon before my stylist books up. Oh yes, the family Christmas card. Have to get that out. Oh, and the tree! Plus all of the decorations: ornaments and ribbons, stockings and wreaths, maybe something new for the front porch. And then there's the office party and all the gifts for the family and friends. Are the in-laws coming over this year? Also need to confirm if we are traveling so I can book flights. We'll need to order a new couch and dining room table, and get the rugs cleaned. The

food! Better make a list, but I don't know where I'll even find the time for grocery shopping. Lights—need those lights up on the house…"

The list goes on and on. BUT WAIT A MINUTE. Who has the proverbial pistol to your head? Where are the Christmas police? Will they fine you for lack of Christmas cheer? Are you going to be arrested for holiday insubordination? Does Santa have it out for you with a one-two punch? Me thinks not. So, who is forcing this holiday stress spiral upon you? That's right—it's you. Take a deep breath and recall

a simpler time. Remember when you were a child, and the holidays held a very different and special meaning for you. Now, **take back your holiday**. Own it. It's yours to enjoy, and it's up to you to make it special—for you.

Now, there are those who will argue that the holidays are supposed to be a time of giving. Owning our holiday makes us selfish, right? Besides, Christmas is more about the children. However, I beg to differ. Since the wisest and most honest people I know are usually under the age of five, perhaps we should turn to them for guidance on how to make the most of our holidays,

rather than use them as an excuse for enduring a self-inflicted Christmas craze.

Those first five years (plus a few more I hope) are the golden years for children where Christmas is truly magical. Kids know and feel everything. They are observant and sensitive, so if mommy or daddy (or any other family member) is completely stressed out and frustrated beyond control, it hardly makes for a joyful time. Providing safety, security, love, a spiritual connection—and a little sprinkling of Santa in just the right places—makes all the difference. These are the memories they will take with them for their rest of their lives. How do we really make these moments special? By showing that we truly are enjoying the holiday season just as much as the children. To do that, we need to own the holiday joy for ourselves. The rest comes easy.

When you ask anyone what they recall as the special part about Christmas, they might briefly talk about one or two extravagant gifts that Santa left under the tree, perhaps that awesome bike with a basket and bell, or that nifty train set that steamed and whistled. But the rest of the time, they share stories about how the holiday was spent celebrating the unique traditions that made it magical: stealing extra pieces of grandma's famous fudge, singing carols by the piano, waking up before sunrise to see if Santa ate the plate of cookies. The joyous feelings inspired by Christmastime celebrations make it a wonderful event, not the bike or the train set. It's time to reconnect with your inner child—heartened by joyous events rather than material things—and bring that kid along for the ride in all that you do this season.

Holiday History
The Santa Factor

He goes by many names, that jolly elusive elf. I'm sure you've heard several of these at one time or another: Father Christmas, Kris Kringle, or Saint Nick. Perhaps you've even heard a few of his illustrious, international titles such as the French 'Pére Noél,' Russia's 'Grandfather Frost,' or 'Sinterklass' from the Dutch. His worldwide renown goes on and on, although little information can be traced back to pinpoint an exact origin.

The broad strokes of Mr. C's existence closely resemble the legend of Saint Nicholas, a patron saint of children and sailors from long, long ago. Kind and giving, he was best known for throwing sacks of money into open windows or down chimneys in homes of the poor. My kind of guy!

Eventually, the celebrated tale grew and transformed this hero from a benevolent saint to a loveable elf. Making its way to America, the legend was first depicted in 1844 with a newspaper drawing of the gift-giver. The nineteenth century was a robust time for all things Christmas; the Victorian era popularized everything from cards to trees and made it a royal big deal.

Santa Claus has been, and most likely will remain, the brand ambassador of holiday happiness. He's managed to inch his way into the hearts and minds of children and adults for generations. The New York Sun newspaper reported that "Yes, Virginia— there is a Santa Claus," back in 1897, and reposted that editorial piece each and every year by popular demand for over 50 years, until the paper finally closed its doors in 1949. The Sun's editor, Francis P. Church, wrote, "How dreary the world would be if there were no Santa Claus." How dreary indeed. Even the U.S. Postal Service confirmed him to be real in the 1947 movie classic, Miracle on 34th Street. Who are we to argue with that?

While we may never know the details of his actual beginnings, we do know that Santa Claus has quite a reputation for bringing wonder to those of us in need of a little Christmas magic.

CHAPTER TWO

Planning Your Season

S ure, reconnecting with your inner kid is one thing, but you're still saying, "How in the world do we enjoy ourselves when there is so much to be done?" Activities and chores seem never-ending during the season. Some of us may actually thrive on the hustle bustle, as it can be part of what makes Christmas grand, while others may want to hide under the bed until Groundhog Day. No matter where you fall on the thrive-to-hide spectrum, a little self-reflection and planning go a long way during the throes of holiday activity.

It's important to remind ourselves that there's no humanly possible way to handle every task. Even though we may know that, intuitively, we still tend to place an enormous amount of pressure on ourselves, which inevitably leads to disappointment. If we try to do too many things at once, everything falls just a little short (or maybe even way short) of how we envision it. Yet, when it comes to Christmas, we hold our breath and tackle our lengthy to-do lists like a linebacker in the big game. Spread yourself too thin and suddenly you feel like the breath's knocked out of you, and rather out of the holiday spirit, the very thing you should be filled with and relish. So, here's the answer—you've got to have a game plan.

Don't worry if you're not a great planner. I'm not talking about charts and graphs to manage the holiday. It's much easier than that.

First, ask yourself what you care about doing most this holiday season. What are your very favorite parts about Christmas? Is it cooking for loved ones? Hosting a great party? Hearing the church choir on Christmas Eve? Decorating the tree? Putting up lights in the front yard? Shopping for gifts? Making cookies? Attending the annual charity drive? You already know in your heart what makes you feel splendid and truly in the spirit of the season. You don't even have to write it down (although it can't hurt)!

Of course, many Christmas traditions and activities hold their own special magic, and having a combination of experiences can create a wonderful, memorable season. But which ones are you going to own and commit yourself to fully, rather than half-heartedly? Limiting the items to just a few can be the hardest part, but like anything else, once you experience the freedom it offers and the joy you gain, you'll never go back.

Now that you have a goal, make a game plan by choosing two or three activities to focus on, and make them yours. Take them to heart. Add your special touches and then share your plan with loved ones. If hosting a great party and decorating cookies made your list, then focus your time and energy on those pursuits. You'll do an incredible job, and your family and friends will be wowed by what you do and will reap the rewards of a joyfully-planned party and tins filled with cheerful home-baked goods.

Next, huddle up with the people you plan to spend the holidays with and talk about the things they want to do or experience. Support them in owning their two or three activities. Now you have a condensed list of pursuits you can all enjoy together with each person dedicated to spearheading a few activities. After all, Christmas is not an isolated experience, and the joy of the season truly shines when everyone gets involved, whether they are neighbors, friends, or family members.

We must give ourselves permission to let go of some things so that we can focus on the holiday activities and traditions that really matter to us. Just like a potluck dinner, a little planning and communication makes for a great meal, without one person trying to cook and feed everyone. The fare is varied and plentiful, and there's more time for all to mingle.

The Christmas Game Plan

The beauty in the Christmas game plan is in having more time to experience the other parts of the season that usually slip away from you each year. More time is key and is what lets you enjoy the season. Picture this …

You've owned the tree and the Christmas cards this year. You've always wanted a themed tree for the house. Special ornaments and a spectacular light display are glowing. You organized the tree trimming night, which was easy, because your spouse handled the cookies, hot chocolate, and invites. He loves to bake and share special treats, and he owned that this year. The Christmas card looks fabulous because you had time to organize the family photo, put together a beautiful card, and even mailed them out early (a much happier ending compared to previous years when boxes of Christmas cards sat stuffed in the corner until you finally threw them away in the spring, because there was just never enough time).

The house looks great because your children owned setting the lights up, and it's a super display. You all opted to forego the usual, intense decorating throughout the house and went Christmas Lite (more on that later ...). What now? Well, there's a bit more time, so why not all get into the car for a drive to see the lights in the neighborhood? How fun!

You get the picture, and isn't it a good one? Less stress, more Christmas joy. Divvying up the holiday must-haves is the best way to stay sane while getting the most out of this very special time of year. Next year, maybe you'll switch up your list to get some exciting variety, or keep it the same to perfect a seamless holiday routine. That's the best part—it's totally up to *you*.

Helpful Holiday Tip

If you're a big Christmas go-getter and dig the challenge, the end of October is the time to set your calendar straight. Right after you pack away your Halloween costume, plan out your weeks right up until the New Year. If you plot out what needs to be done, you won't be as overwhelmed as you would be not knowing what's next on your agenda! Still too much? Cut something out. No one feels very festive when tired and cranky. Bah-humbug!

CHAPTER THREE

Beating Christmastime Stress

You may be thinking, "Wait, Christmas is a time of abundance. Won't limiting traditions and activities take all of that away?" The definitive answer is no. What you are giving up is stress. What you're getting is more time to enjoy the season. That means abundance. That means getting to do more of the things you say you're going to do each year but never get the chance to, because you have a list of 500 other items to get done in roughly three or four weeks. Simple question—would you plan a big wedding or special event in a month's time? You might try, and needless to say that would be stressful, leaving no time for enjoyment during the weeks prior to the big day. And on that big day, you'd be exhausted and would probably poop out way before the shindig ends. The lead up to December 25th is no different.

Think about our usual Christmas expectations: so much planning, running about, doing, all for the big day. During the holidays, we sometimes go through our rituals and traditions in mind-numbing order without ever really knowing why we do what we do. Maybe we do that because that's the way it's always been done. Is that reason enough?

Once the holiday's over, there's a fall from the whirlwind that had us bouncing around, and we tend to feel regretful that we missed the spirit of the season. Imagine the experiences you can have with more time on your hands. Now, let me share with you a few inexpensive, joyous pleasures of the season, and some tips on how to get there.

Getting Into the Spirit

Getting into the holiday spirit begins months before December rolls around. In the fall, stores already start to fill their window displays with everything Christmas, yet autumn still lingers in the air. Why the rush? Can't we take the time to revel in the here-and-now? Leaves change color and fall to the ground as the trees gently brown. The brittle  branches and cool air lend to the perfect Halloween background. Then, the smells of caramel corn and crisp apple pies baking in the oven transport us to Thanksgiving. Yet, retailers can't wait to be kill-joys, rush through these glorious holidays, and skip right to hanging the tinsel.

Let's fight the madness, people. Allow your own holidays to simmer, just like a Dutch oven slowly stewing your warm Indian summer dinner. Let the retailers of the world fool the rest of the folks into early submission; as for us, we'll slow it down and breathe. We'll get there when the time is right.

Thanksgiving is the time to think about turkey, football, and freedom from work. For many, this is *the* favorite holiday, because it connects family and friends without the pressure. There's no requisite gift giving, save the bottle of wine or edible treat that's brought to the family feast. Perhaps there's the annual game of flag football in the front yard. All you have to do is show up and be present to participate in these treasured moments.

Give thanks to the blessings, big and small. Have another slice of pumpkin pie and savor your warm apple cider. Catch up with loved ones. Regale with stories of holidays past. Ask grandparents about their holidays as children and watch their eyes light up as they tell their tales. These small actions serve as the building blocks for the foundation of your holiday season.

After all that fun settles in, we can safely transition to the continuing holiday joy that is Christmastime. This year, you'll arrive without fear or hesitation, rejuvenated and uplifted after fully savoring your fall holidays. It's time to go full throttle into the merriment, not the stress.

Seasonal Side Note: For the record, as a proponent of the one-holiday-at-a-time rule, it's officially legal to begin listening to Christmas music the Friday after Thanksgiving while staying in your pajamas all day.

The Stress Buster

By now, no doubt, you are shaking your head and recalling all the usual errands you normally do each year, the way-too-many plans you make, and the deemed obligatory parties you attend. But not this year. Now that you are taking back your holidays, you won't get bogged down or lost in all the mayhem.

The trick is to enjoy the buildup. If you take the time to enjoy the little moments for each season, it becomes a holiday well spent, one where each bite of festive food and every shared conversation with loved ones leaves a lasting impression in your mind, rather than culminating in another season that simply passed you by because you were too busy to look up.

Early Shopping Time

Shopping early is an incredible stress buster, and you can get a jump on your holiday shopping well before December. One option is to slowly gather gifts throughout the year, setting them aside so that when Christmastime arrives, all you have to do is wrap your closet full of goodies. If buying gifts that far in advance seems daunting, try keeping a list of gift ideas in your phone or in your notebook, so that when it's time to start shopping, you have already saved time and energy on one of the hardest parts of gift giving—thinking of great gift ideas. From there, it's smooth sailing.

Another option is to take advantage of sales during Thanksgiving week. Black Friday is a tradition that some people just can't do without, and the thrill of the chase beckons them. Many stores now open in the evening on Turkey Day, to give you a head start ... or to avoid football ... or to forget about your team's loss. Why go out? Why not! Your tummy is full, you're wide awake after your long, afternoon tryptophan nap, and there are sales going on, people!

Helpful Holiday Tip

Use helpful mobile apps to compare pricing, gather coupons, and scout seasonal sales before you venture out. You'll have a plan and a better handle on your gift buying list and budget.

Seasonal Reminders

Car etiquette

Don't leave packages in plain sight in your car, not even for a little while. It's just not a good idea. The temptation is far too great for someone to break in and take your treasures. Lock everything up in your trunk or place them hidden from view if you must leave items behind.

Keeping cool like Frosty ...

Be patient out there on the road. Christmastime car accidents and fender benders go on the rise during the holiday season, because everyone is in such a hurry. (Not you, of course, because you took back your holidays.) Weather challenges add an extra layer of difficulty. Don't have a holiday mishap and turn the fa la la into "fer cryin' out loud." Slow down for shoppers and the Christmas lights. All those glittering displays are meant to be viewed. Take them all in with someone you love and arrive safely.

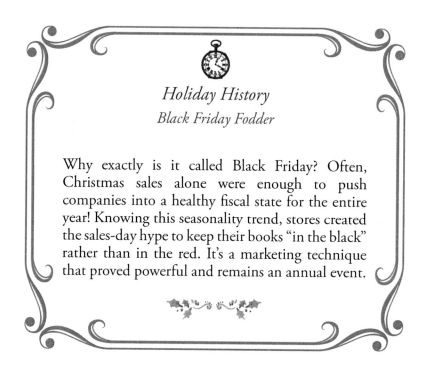

Holiday History
Black Friday Fodder

Why exactly is it called Black Friday? Often, Christmas sales alone were enough to push companies into a healthy fiscal state for the entire year! Knowing this seasonality trend, stores created the sales-day hype to keep their books "in the black" rather than in the red. It's a marketing technique that proved powerful and remains an annual event.

Perhaps you prefer ordering items on Cyber Monday (the Monday after Thanksgiving) and purchasing your gifts online. What a rewarding time saver and stress buster, avoiding long lines or the eternal hunt for a parking space! A little leisurely site browsing and web surfing is a convenient way to shop, and it's  even better if you know exactly what you want and where to get it. Santa's delivery is just a click away!

Helpful Holiday Tip

Returning or exchanging items purchased online that aren't

quite what you had in mind can take time, sometimes weeks. Be sure to do your on-line return research before you buy, in case an item has to be shipped back.

If you're a fan of the malls and all the splendid holiday décor, try to go early in the season to keep stress to a minimum. Making your way through a mall close to Christmas Day is setting yourself up for maximum overload. Planning your mall trips early in the season is always a good idea to keep calm and shop in heavenly peace.

Seasonal Reminder

Stay healthy during the holiday season and avoid a nasty cold. Remember the number one preventive trick— washing your hands often, especially after picking up items in stores that everyone else picked up, too. Can't get to soap and water? Carry hand sanitizer or antibacterial wipes with you.

Schedule the "Me Time"

Above all, don't forget to leave time for yourself. Make an appointment in your calendar for "Me Time" and stick to it. You'll feel better about everything if you reward yourself. Use your "Me Time" for something you really enjoy and don't let anything get in the way. Here are some popular recommendations, but do whatever gives you space to refuel and recharge. Even Santa's elves break for the sunset. Jolly good idea, no?

- *Steal away for a quiet cup of cocoa, specialty coffee, or your favorite beverage.*

- *Sneak in a quiet, warm, winter's nap, even if it's in the car.*

- *Book a small spa treatment.*

- *Attend a favorite sporting event.*

- *Stop and view the lights on your street.*

- *Take in a local holiday festival or concert.*

All in all, remember to take your moments and honor them. Indulge your way. Experience the season. Don't try to be perfect at Christmastime. Have a perfect Christmas instead. Know it will return in a year, like an old friend, waiting for you to experience it once again.

4

··········•❧·· CHAPTER FOUR ·❧·•··········

Priceless Winter Activities

With the extra time gained from taking back your holidays, there's plenty to see and do. And much of it can be enjoyed without spending a small fortune. Sure, these may seem obvious, but I bet some of you can't recall the last time you did one of them, because you were just too busy! Here are a few suggestions to get your holiday merriment on without breaking the Christmas Club account.

- **Go for a ride in the car to see neighborhood lights and decorations.**

  In almost every city, there's a fabulous light display or veritable "Candy Cane Lane." Whether it's city sponsored in a park, or it's a family neighborhood tradition, there surely exists a place to see the lights near you.

- **Take in the local school's holiday musical, concert, or play.**

   Even if your kids are past a young school age or you don't have any children enrolled, you can still attend a school event. Many schools open their seasonal offerings to the community. With a purchase of a ticket that surely won't break the piggy bank, you'll be treated to a heart-warming show and contribute to a worthy cause.

- **Attend a church choir concert.**

   Big bang for your free time with this one. Explore your local church for their choir offerings and celebrations during the season. Even if you don't attend the church regularly, it's a wonderful way to bring in some Christmas cheer.

- **Go caroling.**

   When's the last time you warbled for the neighbors? It's a great excuse to be silly and have fun, without having to be talented!

- **Play in the snow.**

   If you live where the white stuff is plentiful, sledding, building a snowman, or a good old-fashioned snowball fight is marvelous fun.

- **Bake cookies**.

   Nothing says Christmastime like the sweet aroma of cookie dough baking in the oven. Spend quality time with the family and bake a batch together. (Check out chapter six for ways to bust the cookie baking hassles.)

- **Attend your local tree lighting ceremony.**

Being present when your city or town turns on the electric juice is loads of fun for the little ones and not a bad treat for yourself. How can you not smile when beholding a tradition that captures the imagination and spurs feelings of wonder and hope? It's a memorable way to enjoy the season. Along with the tree lighting ceremony, look for Santa visits, petting zoos, or other sponsored events.

- **Have a holiday movie night.**

What a great way to spend a December evening. Load up a favorite Christmas movie, snuggle up under a warm blanket with a big bowl of fresh, buttery popcorn, and enjoy! Plus, you have so many wonderful Christmas movies to choose from, both old and new. From *It's a Wonderful Life*, to *National Lampoon's Christmas Vacation*, and *The Christmas Story*, there's something for everyone in the house.

1983 by MGM/UA Entertainment Co.

21

If you haven't yet enjoyed the original *Miracle on 34th Street* movie, or if it's been a while, place it on the "holiday movie night" list. As a three-time Oscar winner, it's worth the time. While there are many special moments in the film, I always go to my favorite line in the movie: "Christmas isn't just a day, it's a state of mind." Never stated better.

Miracle on 34th Street 1947— Courtesy of 20th Century FOX

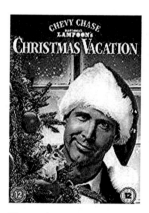

National Lampoons Christmas Vacation: Warner Bros. 1983

Seasonal Side Note: Great holiday movies are plentiful, but if you're looking for recommendations or reminders of familiar favorites, check out my blog for a compiled list of popular choices.

www.drxmas.com

Holiday History
Saving for Christmas

The Christmas Club Account was made popular during the Great Depression years from 1929 through 1939. It was a tough time for everyone, so banks created this special savings account to help customers stash away a little bit each month for Christmastime spending. Banks gave away gifts like small appliances to encourage opening accounts. Nowadays, you can easily set up an automatic savings plan online with your bank for the very same outcome. No need to visit the bank or open another account. Free toaster not included.

CHAPTER FIVE

Decorating with Ease

If you're anything like me, you have enough Christmas decorations to spruce up the entire neighborhood and then some. If decorating is your claim of ownership, have at it! Decorating certainly creates holiday cheer in any home and sets the merry mood.

But if you're looking for a simpler way to deck the halls, use a variety of seasonal greenery. It's the easiest way to bring the holiday feel in without too much work. Use an assortment of poinsettias and wreaths. Hang up a sprig of mistletoe. Grab extra tree cuttings from a tree lot or farm; they're often piled up high and free for the taking. A touch of holly in a glass vase or jar with a red bow shouts Christmastime, and that's all you really need to be in the spirit. Halls decked. Check.

Holiday History
Wreath Magic

That fabulous wreath is probably one of the first items chosen to decorate your home. Whether it's over the mantle or on the door, a wreath welcomes in the season. But why do we do that?

Hanging wreaths on the door relates back to early Greek and Roman days when the victors of athletic challenges received a laurel crown, which was later displayed on the door to represent a trophy, similar to the Olympic medals bestowed upon athletes today. As for the meaning behind the circle of greenery, there isn't one solid straight answer. For some, the circle symbolizes eternity; for others, evergreens that stay verdant through the harsh winter bring fortitude. Wreaths can also reflect religious beliefs as a symbol for preparing to welcome Christ. Whatever your reason for hanging the beautiful ring of greens up, it certainly symbolizes there are festive folk living behind that door! No champion downhill skiing required.

Mistletoe Mayhem

What is this crazy custom about kissing under mistletoe? Why do we do this? And do I really need to give Aunt Bertha a smooch under that doorway where it hangs?

Ah, so much kissing pressure surrounds the mistletoe ritual. Back in the days of yesteryear, if an unwed gal wasn't kissed under the mistletoe during

Christmastime, she'd be set for another year of the single life. Now that's pressure!

But did you know you're really kissing under a 'stick of dung'? Yes, you read that right. Mistletoe is a plant that grows partially by living off other plants. It's parasitic, which basically means it's a big fat leech that uses other plants to survive. One of the ways mistletoe spreads around and grows is by way of birds. They eat the berries and then – ahem--"drop" their own presents onto foliage. The word mistletoe stems from the Old English word 'misteltan'--*mistel* meaning "dung" and *tan* meaning "twig"; literally "dung on a stick." Wherever there were bird droppings, the mistletoe plant was sure to sprout, and that was pretty magical since no one had planted seeds.

Mistletoe has had a lengthy history and has been linked to Norse mythology where it was branded a good luck charm filled with gratitude and love, and more than likely, the root of the romantic love we connect it with today. The Druids believed mistletoe to be a medicinal remedy, healing diseases and protecting against evil spirits and the dark forces of the world. There are many different varieties, but, in general, mistletoe is toxic to humans and pets (oddly enough though, not to birds); it will cause a heck of a tummy ache and can be dangerous, even fatal, if eaten in large quantities. Then again, come to think of it, Aunt Bertha's fruitcake is pretty lethal too (but that's another chapter).

Now, there is a proper way to kiss under the cutting. According to mistletoe etiquette, when a lady under the holiday sprig is kissed, one of the berries must be removed. Once all the berries are gone, the mistletoe is all out of kissing power. You might try telling Aunt Bertha all the berries are gone this year when she comes in for her smack. It may not get you out of the kiss, but at least she'll think you're really smart!

The Poinsettia's Past

Originating in Mexico, the poinsettia is a warm-climate plant which was brought to the U.S. in 1828 by Joel Poinsett (hence the name), who was the ambassador of Mexico. Its bright red color and festive appearance make it truly one of the most notable symbols of the season. It grows in all 50 states, with California as the leading producer of poinsettia plants.

Poinsettias are mistakenly thought of as highly poisonous when in fact they are not. But people and pets can be sensitive to the milky sap substance that oozes from the leaves and flowers. Yes, those bright red petals are actually leaves, and the yellow berry-like cluster center is the flower.

If you live in a warmer climate and want to enjoy that festive greenery next year, hang on to your plant after the holiday, water it sparingly, and leave it in a warm, low-lit area for about a month. Then move it back into sunshine or a well-lit area and resume watering regularly. It'll return to its leafy-red self again next year. And by the way, National Poinsettia Day is December 12th—who knew? Now, you do!

- The Paul Ecke Ranch in California grows over 80 percent of poinsettias in the United States, and 90 percent of the plants worldwide got their start here.

- There are over 100 varieties of poinsettias available.

- $220 million worth of poinsettias are sold during the holiday season.

The Christmas Tree

Every holiday has a symbolic "belle of the ball," and the classic evergreen fits the description, skirt and all. It's the focal point of any home, and, for most, it's just not Christmas without it. There are countless ideas you can bring to life with the tree as your creative masterpiece, from traditional red and gold ornaments to unique themes like beachy seashells. Tree trimmings can be vintage or new, summer travel souvenirs, or handmade treasures. The sky is the limit, so make it your own!

Do you plan on getting the plastic tree out from the garage or selecting a fresh one from a local supplier? Before you make the usual annual move, take a moment to consider which one is right for you this season.

Helpful Holiday Tips

- If you're planning to travel and won't be home much this season, a low-maintenance artificial tree is a better bet than a fresh tree that requires regular watering.

- If you have small children or young pets in the home, a small table-top tree is safer and stays out of reach of curious hands and paws.

- If you have a green thumb and an eco-friendly mindset, choose a live container tree that can be replanted or donated once the season is over.

- If you live in a space-challenged home, create holiday magic even without live greenery by hanging green sticky note paper or a strand of lights to design a wall tree. No square footage lost and you still have a place to tuck a present or two!

Taming the Tree

If fresh, live Christmas tree splendor is calling your name, here are a few tidbits of information to choose a tree wisely and to keep it in peak shape:

- When selecting your tree, gently squeeze the branches to make sure the needles are supple and pliable. This indicates a moist, fresh tree. Avoid those with loose or falling needles.

- Make sure you give it a fresh cut when you get home. Even if it's cut at the tree lot, a new cut at home will allow the tree to soak up the water it needs to stay fresh longer. Sap escapes quickly upon cutting and can form a barrier to keep your tree from 'drinking' up that much needed H_2O.

- Skip the special preservatives and expensive water additives, as most garden experts agree that they're not necessary.

- Water the tree regularly and check its water level often to ensure a fresher tree all season long.

Holiday History
Tree Trimming Trivia

Wonder why we call it "trimming the tree" and where the phrase comes from? During the Victorian era when Christmas trees became fashionable, most were decorated with lace or ribbon. These materials served as the "trim" or edgings of ornate coats and dresses. Thus, it became known as the "tree trim" or the act of trimming the tree.

Helpful Holiday Tip

If you're trying to fix that string of lights because you're sure you can find that ONE bulb that is burnt out, think twice about your value-to-time ratio. Lights are relatively inexpensive and buying new ones is a safe and sane habit. If your strand has seen better tree days, throw it out and opt for a brand-new set.

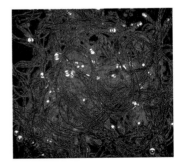

33

Christmas Lite

If there's just no time or energy for 'operation decoration' with a myriad of stored boxes holding yuletide trinkets, relax. Go Christmas Lite (I promised you I'd get to that.) Once again, the Christmas police will not cite you for less than over-the-top décor. Bring empty plastic bins into the house and switch out a few of your current items for holiday favorites. You'll make room for the holiday decor without adding clutter to your current year-round pieces. Go easier this year. You'll never feel a lack of Christmas cheer.

- Don't unbox every single Christmas item you own in the garage for display.

- Be choosy and only bring out a few decorations that have strong meaning to you and your family.

- Trade with your neighbors to add a touch of inspiration and conversation.

- Hang on to the cherished family heirlooms and delicate items, so no one messes with the ornament you made in fifth grade or the ornament grandma gave your child.

- Purchase one new piece to start a fresh tradition.

- Throw out broken or unwanted extra ornaments.

Helpful Holiday Tips

Be sure to tag and mark your decoration boxes to make storage easier when it's time to box them up. Reference what's *in* the box on the outside so that you know what you're opening, i.e., "Christmas Tree Ornaments" or "Outside Lights." Keep tissue paper and packaging materials in the box for faster repacking.

Keep ornament hooks on ornaments and gently pack them away after the season. (You'll be thrilled come Christmastime again with ready-to-be-hung decorations.)

Seasonal Reminder

One year, Mom accidentally gave a box of cherished family tree ornaments from our garage to a local charity. Luckily, Mom caught her mistake and quickly realized there was a missing box thanks to her handy tagging system. She rushed to the shop, found the decorations, and bought them all back before they were lost forever. Long story short, be sure to mark your boxes! It's a huge time saver and prevents accidental removal mishaps.

6

Christmas in the Kitchen

Nothing says Christmastime like rich, warm smells wafting from the kitchen. An oven filled with seasonal delights is a present all by itself and worth the baking-time wait. For the happy cook who loves to bake during the holidays, this is pure holiday joy! But a tip or two up one's sleeve (or apron) can assist even the most experienced Christmas baker.

Baking with ease

- Grab a tray and gather all your usual baking ingredients, such as baking soda, baking powder, flour, sugar, extracts, nuts, chocolates, and spices.

- Place the tray on the counter, in your pantry, or on a shelf.

- Check for ingredients you might be running low on and add them to the list for the next shopping trip.

- When you are ready to bake, all items will be waiting for you in one convenient portable place. No more wild searches for hidden or absent ingredients.

Seasonal Tip

Here's an easy, no-fuss way to make the house smell like Christmas with ingredients you probably have on hand. There are no hard-and-fast rules here; experiment with some of your favorite scents to get the recipe just right for your nose.

Gently simmer the following in 1 quart of water:

3 cinnamon sticks
¼ cup whole cloves
1 teaspoon ground cloves
½ cup fresh cranberries
Orange and lemon slices (2-3) slices
½ teaspoon nutmeg
Be sure to add more water as needed while it simmers.
Additional options: pine sprigs, star anise, or rosemary.

Holiday History
Fruitcake Anyone?

What is the deal with this "beloved" and time-honored holiday pastry? I bet you don't know a single person who enjoys receiving a fruitcake gift. And even if you are one of the rare ones who really enjoys a good slice with a warm holiday beverage, why do we eat this stuff mainly during the holidays?

The real tradition dates all the way back to the 13th century when dried fruits and nuts were imported into Britain and were added to dough to enhance the flavor of bread. Viewed as a great way to preserve fresh fruits and nuts, the items were encased in sugar, alcohol, and a heavy batter to make it all stick together. All that buttery egg and flour mix make the cake very dense, heavy enough to serve as a door stopper or self-defense tool.

Back in the good ole days when the local grocery store wasn't an option, fruitcakes took an enormous amount of time and energy to bake, making it a genuine labor of love. Churning butter, grinding the finest flour, adding rose water, all of these details were meticulously heeded in order to create the perfect offering to friends, family, and the poor.

Carolers in the bitter cold were offered fruitcake in exchange for their gift of song. It traveled well, made a solid meal for an empty tummy, and lasted through the harsh winters. From there, it developed a life of its own as a tradition that just won't go away. In any case, the fruitcake has been around a long time. And I bet the one in your cupboard has too (some fruitcakes have a known shelf life of about 25 years)!

Some traditions were meant to be broken.

Christmas Cookies - Tips and Tricks

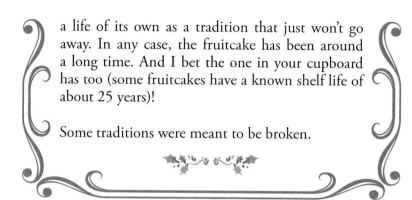

- Always pre-heat your oven when baking.

- When in doubt, 350° degrees is a reliable temperature for most recipes.

- Keep the kitchen at room temperature whenever possible, along with your eggs and butter if the recipe calls for them.

- Prep and measure all your ingredients first, so you never mess up your recipe. The French call it 'mise en place' (MEEZ ahn plahs) for "everything in its place." *Tres bien, oui?*

- Mix your wet ingredients and dry ingredients well separately before combining.

- Don't bake cookies when it's raining or snowing heavily if you can help it! Too much moisture can affect the outcome.

The Holiday Cookie Hack

One can never have enough Christmas cookie recipes! But these recipes are extra special. Not only are they delicious, but they make holiday munching 'munch' easier. With make-ahead and freeze-for-later instructions, you can have all the fun of Christmas cookie making before the holiday visitor traffic arrives, leaving you one less thing to juggle when the season gets busy. Pick a day, make the dough with loved ones, maybe bake a batch for yourself to enjoy fresh out of the oven, and freeze the rest. Once the busy holiday season is in full swing, you'll be prepped for easy-bake homemade cookies anytime! Just pull the dough out of the freezer, thaw, cut, and bake. There's even a no-bake recipe for the ultimate shortcut.

These great recipes courtesy of personal chef, Tracy McWain, owner of Total Local Chef: www.totallocalchef.com who's a dynamo in the kitchen.

Chocolate Crinkle Christmas Cookies

Yields about 30 cookies

<u>Ingredients</u>
4 tablespoons butter (1/4 cup)
4 oz. unsweetened baking chocolate, melted
2 cups granulated sugar
2 teaspoons vanilla extract
4 eggs
2 cups all-purpose flour
2 teaspoons baking powder
½ teaspoon salt
1 cup powdered sugar

Preparation:
In a large, heavy saucepan over low heat, melt butter and chocolate, stirring occasionally until smooth. Remove from heat and transfer to a bowl.

Stir sugar into warm chocolate mixture. Add eggs, one at a time, beating well after each addition. Sift in flour, baking powder, and salt. Stir until smooth. Cover and refrigerate, two to three hours or overnight.

Photo by Traci McWain,
Total Local Chef

Baking:
Preheat oven to 300° degrees
Adjust two racks to divide oven into thirds. Line cookie sheets with parchment paper or use silicone baking mats to prevent the cookies from sticking.

Place powdered sugar in a small bowl. Rub powdered sugar on the palms of your hands and roll dough into 1 1/2-inch balls. Roll each ball around in the bowl of powdered sugar and place 2-inches apart onto prepared cookie sheets.

Bake 20 to 22 minutes or until tops of cookies are barely semi-firm to touch—the centers should be slightly soft. Reverse position of sheets top to bottom and front to back once during baking to ensure even baking. (If you bake only one sheet at a time, place the pan on the higher rack.) Remove from oven and cool on wire racks.

Storing: These cookies will keep in an airtight container for up to three days or in the freezer for up to two months. Sprinkle with fresh confectioners' sugar after thawing.

Freezing Dough: Roll dough into balls and freeze on a cookie sheet (skip the powdered sugar for now) and then store in sealable freezer bags. When ready to bake, remove as many cookie balls as you need from the freezer and let thaw for 30 minutes. Then, roll each cookie in powdered sugar and bake according to the directions above.

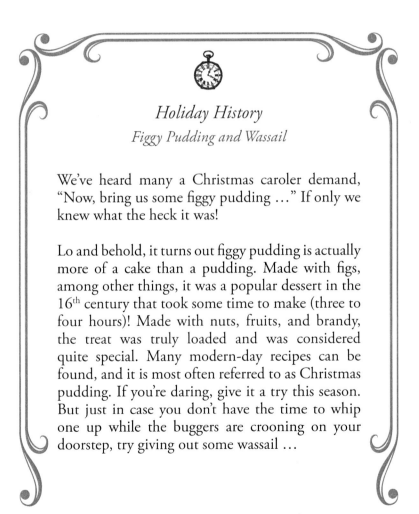

Holiday History
Figgy Pudding and Wassail

We've heard many a Christmas caroler demand, "Now, bring us some figgy pudding …" If only we knew what the heck it was!

Lo and behold, it turns out figgy pudding is actually more of a cake than a pudding. Made with figs, among other things, it was a popular dessert in the 16th century that took some time to make (three to four hours)! Made with nuts, fruits, and brandy, the treat was truly loaded and was considered quite special. Many modern-day recipes can be found, and it is most often referred to as Christmas pudding. If you're daring, give it a try this season. But just in case you don't have the time to whip one up while the buggers are crooning on your doorstep, try giving out some wassail …

Wassail

What? Don't know what that is either? Wassail is an old Germanic term loosely translated to "be healthy," close to our modern day "cheers." We've also heard the rousing rendition of "Here we come a-caroling." Prior to *"a-caroling"* it was *"a-wassailing,"* but some say this lyric was changed due to the frowning-upon of alcohol consumption with caroling visits in England during the middle of the 19th century. So, even though they say they came to sing, they really came to drink! Sounds like a party to me …

You can easily make wassail for you and the carolers. Acquire some ale (any good ale will do). Then, cook up a mixture of apples and pears with sugar, cinnamon, nutmeg, ginger, and cloves, and smash it all together. Add the smashed fruit and spice mixture to the ale, and you've got yourself a warm nectar for the warblers.

Ultimate Sugar Cookies

Yields about 36 cookies

Ingredients:
3 cups all-purpose flour
(plus extra for rolling)
¾ teaspoon kosher salt
½ teaspoon baking powder
1 ¼ cup cold butter (2 ½ sticks)
cut into cubes
1 cup sugar
1 large egg
1 large egg yolk
1 teaspoon vanilla extract

Christmas Cookies Always Delight...

Preparation:
In a small bowl, whisk or sift flour, salt, and baking powder; set aside.

Using an electric mixer on high speed, cream the sugar by adding the cubes of butter one at a time until the sugar and butter are completely combined and creamy. Add the egg, then the egg yolk, then vanilla, combining well after each addition. Reduce speed to low and add flour mixture a little at a time until completely combined.

Remove dough from mixing bowl and divide into two ¾ inch-thick disks. Wrap in plastic wrap and chill at least 2 to 3 hours. For best results, allow your dough to chill overnight.

Baking:
Preheat oven to 325° degrees Once your dough has been properly chilled, remove one disk of dough and let it sit at room temperature for about 5 minutes to soften. On a floured surface, roll out the dough until about ¼ inch thick,

dusting with flour as needed. Cut out shapes with floured cookie cutters and transfer to parchment-lined baking sheet. Bake cookies, rotating baking sheets halfway through, until edges are golden brown, about 8 to 10 minutes depending on cookie size. Transfer to wire rack to cool and repeat with remaining dough. Baked cookies should be completely cooled before decorating.

Make Ahead: Dough can be made and put in freezer for up to one month—place the raw dough disks on a pan in the freezer until frozen and transfer to a sealable freezer bag for storage. Cookies can be baked and frozen up to two months (without decorations).

Decorating with Royal Icing

Ingredients:
3 ½ cups powdered sugar
2 large egg whites

Instructions:
Using an electric blender or stand mixer on medium-high speed, beat sugar and egg whites until thick and tripled in volume.

Add water by the tablespoonful until icing no longer holds a peak and falls like a ribbon.

Divide icing into small bowls and add food coloring. Place colored icing in pastry bags if desired and get creative.

Have fun! (Yes, that's a required step.)

Storing: Once cookies have been decorated and set (this can take anywhere from 3 hours to overnight depending on how much royal icing is used to decorate), place in air tight containers or storage bags. Cookies should stay crisp and fresh for up to 5-7 days.

Holiday History
To Nog or Not to Nog

Let's face it, you either love the drink or hate it, or perhaps you have never even brought yourself to try it (yes, a few of you still remain). The holiday season always brings certain items to grocery store shelves, and eggnog is no exception. But the store-bought kind usually leaves out a key ingredient—alcohol!— and perhaps also leaves a little to be desired. Basic ingredients are milk or cream, eggs, alcohol, and a few spices, usually cinnamon and nutmeg.

Mixed theories exist about the creation and naming of eggnog, but most will agree that the drink probably originated in England where milk and dairy were products belonging to the wealthy. Those with means mixed the finest wines and brandy with dairy products, creating a highbrow punch. Well, everyone wants to be part of the in-crowd, so when English customs made their way to America, where cows and eggs were plentiful, rum was added so that all could partake.

One theory states that the "nog" part of its name developed from the Old English word "noggin" which referred to a carved wooden drinking cup found in taverns. Another school of thought is that rum was commonly referred to as "grog" in early America. If you drank egg with grog in a noggin all night long, you'd be calling it "eggnog" too.

Enjoy that cold glass of your uncle's best-spiced eggnog recipe that's been handed down for generations. And if you hear Rocky bells, but don't quite feel the need to swallow raw egg, fear not! There are plenty of cooked eggnog recipes floating around—in case that makes you feel better about giving it a whirl. Calorie load is on the heavy side, so beware, all of you health conscientious folk. Or at least vow to work off the calories by chasing a chicken. Hey, it worked for Balboa! And if you don't know who Rocky Balboa is, you are definitely too young to be drinking your uncle's famous eggnog.

Whether you make your own or get it already prepared, with alcohol or not, it'll get you eggsactly where you want to be this season—eggstatic, eggcited, egg ... oh just go eggs-periment with this timeless concoction.

Kevin's Kicky Boozy Eggnog

For those of you who need a little kick in your nog, this recipe is sure to please. I know that because my awesome hairdresser slipped it my way. Thanks Kevin! After dealing with holiday coifs all day long, he's bound to need a drink.

Yields 5 quarts

Ingredients:
1 dozen eggs
1-pint whole milk (2 cups)
1 ½ quarts heavy whipping cream
1 ½ cups granulated sugar
1 cup brandy
1-quart Jack Daniels Tennessee Whiskey (4 cups)
2 medium size and 1 extra-large mixing bowls

Directions:
Separate eggs (egg yolks in medium bowl, egg whites in extra-large bowl).

Whip egg yolks until creamy, gradually adding 1/2 cup sugar and 1 cup brandy.

In extra-large bowl, beat egg whites into stiff peaks while adding 1/2 cup sugar.

In third bowl (medium-size), mix 1/2 quart of cream and 1/2 cup sugar to very firm consistency. Set stiff cream aside.

In extra-large bowl of whipped egg whites, fold in yolks,1 pint of whole milk,1 quart of Jack Daniels, and stiff cream.

Funnel into bottles or jars with lids and let sit in refrigerator for at least 24 hours and up to a week, shaking each bottle daily (keeps fresh up to a full year).

No-Bake Chocolate Peanut Butter Cookies

Yields 36 cookies

Ingredients:
2 cups sugar
½ cup cocoa powder
½ cup milk
¼ cup butter
3 cups rolled oats
½ cup peanut butter

Photo by Traci McWain,
Total Local Chef

Directions:
Lay out parchment or wax paper on a clean surface.

In a quart pot on medium-high heat, mix sugar, cocoa powder, milk, and butter until melted and creamy. Bring mixture to a rolling boil for ONE MINUTE ONLY (be careful not to over or under boil). Remove from heat and stir in oats and peanut butter. Mix well until completely combined.

This mixture will be very hot so carefully use two teaspoons to remove and drop 1 ½ inch balls onto parchment paper. The cookie should harden within 10-15 minutes after dropping on the parchment paper. Storing: Cookies will keep in an airtight container for up to a week or in the freezer for up to two months!

Holiday History
The Cool Yule Log Cake

Ah, so many jokes, so little time … and the yule log is always a good mainstay for a holiday chuckle. Why do we have a cake in the form of a brown log in the middle of the holiday buffet table? There are many different takes on the tradition, but it seems fairly safe to say that you can blame the Germans for it. And there are a whole lot of important elements that go along with properly celebrating the super stump.

As early as the 1800s, the man of the house would drag a very large log home to be placed in the hearth when wintertime arrived. The type of wood selected would bring forth different magical properties such as ash for protection, prosperity, and health or birch for new beginnings. This log could never be bought and needed to come from the homeowner's land or received as a gift.

Once placed in the hearth, the log was decorated by the family with flowers and seasonal greenery. In some homes, ale and cider were sprinkled on the log, and wishes were made for the upcoming new year. It was lighted with kindling saved from the previous year's log and ceremoniously roared for Christmas, then smoldered on for 12 days after until finally being doused.

Gradually through the years, as open hearths were replaced with better cooking wares and stove setups, a smaller decorated log was moved to the kitchen table so as not to completely forget the ritual. That explains the proliferation of edible treats in the form of logs at your grocery store.

Now you can take a slab of that holiday woody-looking treat this year and make a wish!

7

Tips on Gift Giving

O h, what to give, what to give? For those of you who just
aren't blessed with gift giving prowess and feel the headache
already, try something different this year. Rather than running
around at the last minute, stealing gifts from under the tree and
re-tagging them, try giving it just a little bit of thought. Not
much, mind you, but just enough to reflect upon the person
you are giving to for a few minutes.

Instead of stressing about conjuring up the perfect gift that is the be-all and end-all (that's way too much pressure) think about the person's lifestyle and go for the obvious. You'd be surprised how many of us don't have the things we'd like for our own hobbies or daily activities. If your friend likes to bike, how about a traveling tire pump or a bike accessory? If your aunt loves the movies, how about a couple of movie tickets from her favorite theatre? And if your boss is a bookworm, how about a book light or a fancy bookmark? Even if your friends and family do own any of these things, chances are they are due for an upgrade, or can never have enough of their favorite things. You get the idea.

The fun part is that the more you know the person, the easier gift giving becomes. Staying simple and focusing on the person leads to the best gifts. In other cases, though, you may not know the person well or may be part of a "pull-a-name" gift exchange. In these situations, nobody will expect something grand or personal, so a gift card or simple seasonal candy treat that can be shared is always a safe choice.

You really can do all your shopping the night before at the local drugstore if you have to, I promise! (More on that later.) But if you'd really like a stress-free holiday, shop early. You don't have to get everything all at once. Spread out your list and enjoy the hunt while eliminating hasty purchases.

One Word. Toys!

Hit the toy stores early for optimum stress-free splendor and great gift-giving options. You'll be reminded of the magic of Christmas as you walk up and down those aisles and will have the time and space to savor the experience. You might even see your favorite toys as a kid lining the shelves and taking you for a trip down memory lane (but prepare yourself to be shocked at how many Barbies and superhero action figures there are these days and the number on the price tag). Or you might come across something that makes you think, "Why didn't they make THAT when I was a kid?" All in all, it's still one of the best places to remember the little kid who lives inside your head and heart, which is something that is truly a Christmas season gift.

If giving toys is high on your list with children and young ones, tackle that early. Nothing's worse than the hottest toy of the season being out of stock and on back-order until January. Don't forget to pick up batteries while you're out, because a toy that doesn't work Christmas morning is bad news …

The good news is toys are relatively inexpensive and a wonderful gift idea, and not just for the little ones! Everyone needs a good game for Wine Night or the neighborhood get-together. While you're there, you can pick out a toy for your local toy drive or company charity event. If it's late in the season and toy stores are much too crowded for your liking, great selections and deals can be found at discount warehouse stores such as Costco and Sam's Club.

Multiple Gift Buying

For some, the office or co-worker dilemma can be a real challenge. If focusing on a lifestyle is way too much work for some folks on your list, try buying in bulk. (Who says too much of a good thing is not a good thing?) While you're out shopping, if something catches your eye and is a great deal to boot, buy several of them. You'll thank yourself later. Going back to find an item that is sold out or picked over is never fun, and the multiple great items will come in handy for group gifting.

Specialty Stores for Thoughtful Gifts

Avoid the malls if you don't like the hustle bustle and go to local stores that don't have long lines or parking nightmares. Hit up the movie theaters or museums for gift certificates and annual passes. Try stopping in that gourmet cheese store, deli, or specialty food shop you pass each day on the way to work and pick up some yummy treats as a gift.

Use your daily errands as a place to knock off a few items. At the car wash or auto shop? Grab some gift cards for a free car wash or oil change. Getting your hair or nails done? Pick up your favorite beauty products or a mani-pedi certificate. Making a stop at the coffee shop? Add a couple of handy travel mugs or gift card to your order. You get the idea.

Recall any favorite things you discovered this past year. Maybe you found a fantastic beauty product that has changed your skin or purchased a sports item this year that has made you a fan. Why not repurchase and share those gifts? They are sure to be a hit for someone who loves your style or shares your activities.

········· **CHAPTER EIGHT** ·········

Christmas Gifting on a Budget

I f gift-giving has gotten you down through the years, and you just want to put a stop to the whole thing, it's time to really pause and think about what the holiday is about. Perhaps it's time to join with the family and friends and talk about a new way of gift giving for the holiday this year. Even though we know gifts are not what Christmas is about, we tend to do the same thing each season (and it is not a nice surprise when the bills come to haunt you at the beginning of the new year). Take charge before you spend money you don't have.

There are many ways to limit spending. First (and often the most overlooked) is to set a personal spend limit. This takes committed planning and ultimately requires really sticking to your list of gift recipients. Give yourself a reasonable range for your standards and allow a little wiggle room for any surprises that may pop up, but be diligent. Letting your budget get away from you is a sure way to have your happy Christmas bubble burst by Christmas trouble.

Set a price limit for each gift. Having your own benchmark can help you with that budget you've established. Share a price cap with your family and friends if possible. This can be tough for those who have a great sense of shopping expertise and finding incredible deals, versus those who aren't as polished, but establishing a top spend per gift sets do-able boundaries. Establish the gift spend limit and have fun really thinking about what your lucky recipient might cherish. Again, it's not about the amount of money you spend, but about connecting with the person to whom you're giving. If you're not sure, ask someone who really knows about that person's likes and tastes—a little effort for a fabulous outcome.

The Name Game (aka Secret Santa)

Pulling names from a Santa hat while gathered around the Thanksgiving table is a great way to start the Christmas present shopping season. Everyone chooses a name and keeps it a secret, allowing for even more excitement and build up to the big reveal.

Can't all be together at Thanksgiving? You can still assign names with easy apps like Elfster. With just an email address and some easy initial set-up, Elfster will deliver your gift recipient's name right to your inbox with no one the wiser—a great way to keep it a secret if that's the plan. Along with a set gift value, no one breaks the bank and everyone concentrates on their named recipient. Win-win!

Work or Club Gift Exchanges

Exchanges are a great solution for gift-giving with large groups. In addition to Secret Santa, the white elephant gift exchange (aka Yankee Swap) offers a fun way for groups to give gifts; each person contributes one wrapped item (which could be anything, ranging from silly socks to practical cookware), and each member of the group takes a turn either unwrapping a present or stealing another person's present. The goal is more about entertainment rather than perfect gifts, inspiring some relaxed fun and a nice break from the normal work grind.

Whichever exchange your group decides to do this season, make sure to communicate with organizers and planners so that everyone is comfortable with the exchange spending limit and is clear about the ground rules. Opt for light-hearted fun and easy sentiments rather than perfect present giving. Or get the company involved with a charitable act in lieu of purchasing gifts this year. It's all about the group and comfort levels. Communication is key!

Themed Gift Giving

Families, friends, and groups can certainly get creative with gift giving by setting a theme for gift exchanges. Some sample exchanges can center around an agreed upon investment level and staying within themed ideas, such as:

- A $20 value with all gifts purchased from a thrift shop or local community store.

- All gifts to be centered around one theme such as music, books, poetry, photographs, or nature.

- All gifts need to be handmade.

- All gifts are acts of service—coupons to clean a room, take out the trash, babysit, or make a meal.

Themed gift giving is a great way for children to feel included and creative, learning about the sentiment rather than focusing on the sticker price. Of course, some families may limit exchanges to adults so that they can stick to the rules for each other, while generously giving to the young ones in the end. As long as the giving is filled with good holiday spirit, it's bound to be a fun time for all!

The Great Stocking Stuffer Challenge

Hanging a stocking on the mantle (or anywhere for that matter) is a wonderfully exciting tradition. Wondering what's going to be in that stocking is half of the fun leading up to the big day, but some folks seem to struggle with what to put in them. After all, it can get a little expensive with a big stocking. (Mom was a big fan of putting fruit and nuts in ours—apples, oranges, and walnuts took up a lot of toe room!)

Stockings are a great way to deliver small, special gifts with heartfelt sentiments. They can be low-key and inexpensive, yet very jolly, such as candy, key chains, small toys, fun socks, yo-yos, or anything you'd pick up at the drug or dollar store. If you have teens or kids off at college, they always appreciate school supplies, gum, and sundries for the dorm room or apartment. There are no rules when it comes to filling stockings, so get creative!

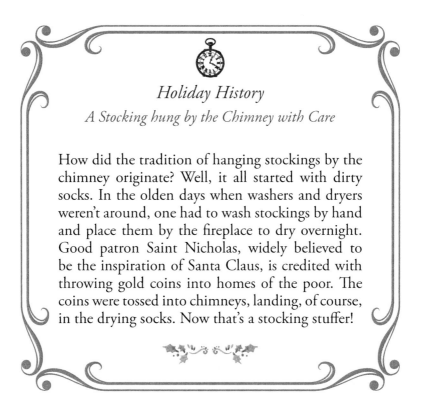

Holiday History
A Stocking hung by the Chimney with Care

How did the tradition of hanging stockings by the chimney originate? Well, it all started with dirty socks. In the olden days when washers and dryers weren't around, one had to wash stockings by hand and place them by the fireplace to dry overnight. Good patron Saint Nicholas, widely believed to be the inspiration of Santa Claus, is credited with throwing gold coins into homes of the poor. The coins were tossed into chimneys, landing, of course, in the drying socks. Now that's a stocking stuffer!

Putting Your Own Hobby to Use

I have a friend who is just wonderful with growing herbs, and each year, I get a little potted herb garden to keep inside and enjoy. It's one of my most treasured presents. Think about what you can offer from your favorite talent and hobby.

- Enjoy taking pictures? Gift a copy of one of your favorites in a fun, inexpensive frame.

- Have a green thumb? Offer one of your blooming bests or wrap up seeds and a few basic garden tools in a pot to get your recipient started.

- Craft your own beer or can your own fruits and veggies? Share a few bottles of your specialty brew or jars of your favorite preserves.

- Paint, sketch, sew, or knit? Share your artistic, handmade goods.

Your inner talent is unique and highly personal. Sharing what you love to do or create with others is a terrific way to really give. It's incredibly special for your recipient to receive a little piece of magic handcrafted by you. If you like the idea of a handmade gift but aren't too handy yourself, look for affordable handmade gifts at craft fairs or online.

Really stuck for a present? Take five minutes to write all the adjectives about your friend or loved one in a holiday card. This simple gesture can transform a store-bought card into a precious, thoughtful keepsake. Or how about a coupon good for a day of shopping together at the after-Christmas sale or going out for lunch? Nothing is more precious than shared time together.

If you are getting closer to the final countdown days before Christmas and still scratching your head wondering what to get others, giving to a charity can be the perfect option. Whether you choose your favorite organization or let the recipient choose, giving to a charitable cause is always a winning bet. Write up a nice card telling your lucky person that you've made a contribution in his or her name. Or, you can send a note asking the recipient to tell you their favorite charity, letting them know you will donate on their behalf this holiday season. This is especially great for the guy or gal who has it all.

Affordable Party Ideas

Now that you have the gift ideas handled, there still might be the task of putting together the Christmas party at the office or the neighborhood gathering at your place. How can you add a special touch to a Christmas party without a lot of Christmas craze and cash?

Host a Hot Chocolate Party

Making a large batch of cocoa or hosting a simple "add hot water and packet mix" mingle is simple and charming. Holiday mugs are everywhere and very reasonably priced. Party goers can make their own hot chocolate by adding toppings from a hot cocoa bar: candy canes, chocolate sprinkles, whipped cream, cinnamon sticks, and a variety of liqueurs to add a little spice. As an added touch, they get to take home the mug they are drinking from as the party gift. Reduced clean-up duty for you and bonus treats for your guests.

Instant Tree Trimming

Some family traditions call for decorating the tree very close to or right before Christmas Day. If you've got a tree that's calling for decorations, but the gift buying has you a little lean on holiday schillings, throw a tree trimming party. Have each guest bring one ornament, store-bought or hand-made, as a party entry ticket. A little music, a few easy seasonal snacks, and your tree and party cheer will be a sight to behold.

Photo Fun

Ask your guests to email a photo of their younger selves at Christmastime, (they may have already shared a few with you on social media). Print copies of the pictures on any white paper and when your guests arrive, be ready with blank cards, envelopes, scissors, some glue sticks, and colorful pens. If you're crafty, bring out that box of stickers and glitter! Party goers will have a blast sharing their youthful Christmas stories and making cards. These make wonderful party favors for your guests to keep or give to a loved one.

PJs and Popcorn

In charge of the kids for an evening? Pajama parties and Christmas stories are amazing ways to create the spirit of the season: writing letters (or emails) to Santa, drawing Christmas cards, popping and stringing popcorn (with some to munch on, of course). There are so many ways to entertain children during the holidays without spending money (but that's a whole other book).

9

Charity: The Greatest Gift of All

What is the meaning of the season without the greatest gift of all? Charity. For many, it may bring to mind the image of us digging deep into our pockets, but giving away dollars may not make much sense in an economically challenging time. For those who have the ability to give, I salute you. Your charity is certain to be a blessing for those in need. For those who find it difficult to find space in the budget for any monetary donations, don't forget that many charitable acts come at little to no cost.

Random acts of kindness during this hustle bustle time can really charge your battery and give you that warm glow, which is what the season is all about.

- Hold a door open for someone with packages.

- Pay a small parking fee for the car behind you.

- Feed an expired meter.

- Leave just a little bigger tip than you normally would.

- Save hotel bottles of shampoo, conditioner, and soap, and donate them to your local shelters.

- Send some old blankets or pet supplies to the SPCA or your local animal shelter.

- Visit a retirement home or children's hospital.

- Donate gently-used clothing or toys.

- Say hello to someone you don't know.

- Volunteer at a local organization, such as the food bank.

The charitable acts are endless, and I'm sure you can think of some not on this list. The more connected you are to your charitable endeavor, the greater the reward.

Part of a larger group that wants to get involved with a charitable cause this season? Pull together to purchase gifts for adopt-a-family charities.

They find families in need and provide lists of requested items from the family members making gift-gathering easier. These services allow these families to enjoy the holiday while getting back on their feet from health issues, lost jobs, or just a run of bad luck or struggles.

Looking for a charitable event the whole family can do together? Get the kids involved early in the season by having them clean out their rooms with one box for trash and another box for donating to either a local hospital or other selected organization of their choice. Soon, gently-used toys and clothing will be ready for gifting. But don't stop there. Have the kids join you on the donation trip and let them truly get involved and see what their generosity breeds. This is bound to turn into a holiday tradition for the entire family. With so many worthwhile causes and needy organizations, you're sure to find the perfect fit for your family.

Be sure to take the time to research your charity organization to make sure they're the real deal. Ask friends and co-workers for recommendations or any groups they might be affiliated with, such as churches, teen help services, or homeless shelters. Many corporations align themselves with specific foundations, so check with your human resources department at work to see if your company supports or sponsors a particular charity. Do a little digging, and you'll truly feel the blessings of the season with your generous offerings.

Holiday History
King "What's-his-name" and a Feast?

Good King Wenceslas looked out
On the feast of Stephen
When the snow lay round about
Deep and crisp and even ...

Who is this king dude and what's the party all about?
Turns out King Wenceslas was a real kindhearted
Czech king who was big on charity. He often
visited the poor, bringing food, money, and other
necessities to beat the harsh winters, and brought
his "page" around with him to help. They gave to
the poor during the Feast of Stephen, a holiday
around the 26th of December that recognizes St.
Stephen, an early martyr of Christianity.

This is where the legend gets good. It was said that
as Wenceslas visited families, trekking through the

bitter cold snow, warmth and light illuminated from his footprints wherever he stepped, allowing the freezing, tired page to follow and continue on with him.

Unfortunately, the kindness gene missed his sibling, and Wenceslas was done in by his own jealous brother. To honor the poor slain do-gooder king, a poem was written which was later set to music. And there you have it.

Oh sure, you may still not know all the lyrics, but at least when you are humming this catchy tune, you'll be reminded of the charity you can offer this season. And you probably won't even have to cross any frozen tundra to do it.

CHAPTER TEN

Holiday Wrapping

My friends and family usually pile up the gifts high at my place and ask me to do my thing—I adore wrapping and own it. But let's face it, many of us just aren't good at wrapping presents, don't like to wrap, or simply don't have the time or patience to complete the package presentations. If any of this applies to you, take heart. There are options!

Let me remind you of the very best tricks:

- *Use the bag method.* Holiday bags are readily available in every store and come in a variety of shapes and sizes. They are easy to find in discount stores and work great for any item. (This is a great time to pull out all the bags you bought at a discount after Christmas last year.)

- *Try a charity wrapping table at your local mall.* If you have a favorite charity or local drive that could use some help with donations, organize your own charity wrapping event early in the season. It's a great way to earn money for a worthy cause or school organization.

- *Enlist younger family members or youthful helpers to assist* and pay a small wage for their efforts. It's a great way for them to earn a little Christmas cash themselves while making your Christmas that much merrier.

- *Host a wrap party.* Gather a group of friends at your place for music and merriment. Supply the paper and ribbons along with tape and scissors or ask your guests to bring some along to assist. In exchange for their elf labor, order pizza and uncork a bottle of wine. Turn up the Christmas songs and provide some holiday treats to munch while wrapping. Soon the conversation will be flowing and the wrapping will be done in no time. Just be sure to keep any gifts for your wrapping crew out of site.

That's a Wrap

If you find yourself running low on a few materials to finish wrapping your treasures, a few of these tips can come in handy:

In need of a ribbon because there are simply no more to be found in the house?

- Shred a few pieces of wrapping paper, gather it on top, and secure it to the package with some tape. Instant Christmas tassels!

- Add a candy cane, a small ornament, or some packages of hot chocolate mix. Voila!

- Use a bit of foliage. A sprig of holly or any greenery you can find, real or faux, looks so festive on a package, even if it is wrapped in a brown paper bag. Done and done!

No more wrapping paper?

- Paper grocery or lunch bags make for great wrapping when the paper roll is empty. Cut one seam of the bag and turn it inside out. Have the kids get out their crayons and draw pictures of Santa, snowflakes, a Christmas tree, or any winter scene they can conjure up. (You might just love these wrappings more than the store-bought paper.)

- If you're a fan of sewing, use extra material on hand or cloth to fold over a present, tie the ends, and tuck in the corners.

- Use foil. It's shiny, durable, and folds neatly around square boxes.

Do You See What I See?

Oh, so much cheer to spread and just never enough time. If you have busy days ahead trying to play Santa and deliver packages yourself during the season, nothing can be more frustrating than trying to locate gifts under the tree. You wrapped it, for Pete's sake, and you know it's there somewhere! You have a pit stop at the Cratchit's house to deliver some gifts, the office party at 6 pm, and dinner with the cousins at 8 pm. If you envision yourself scurrying under the tree, pulling packages out willy-nilly, attempting to read the tags on them, stop the madness this year!

Get inventive, creative, and even, dare you think it, smart. Pick one color or design for each gig—maybe red paper for the Cratchit's, that great blue snowman-patterned paper for the office, and all the green-ribboned gifts for the cousins. Just a bit of forethought goes a long way. The gifts will be easy to find under the tree and you'll be able to throw them in a bag and be out the door, knowing you've got the right gifts. Genius.

·············**❧**·*CHAPTER ELEVEN*·**❧**·············

Those Nifty Christmas Carols

Whatever you might find yourself owning and doing during the season, listening to Christmas carols may be just what the doctor ordered to complete the mood. While tuning in on the car radio, streaming a holiday playlist, popping in your favorite CD, or unwittingly getting trapped in the mall or grocery store with holiday tunes emanating from the rafters, you may wonder, what the heck does that one song mean anyway? Where did that crazy tune come from?

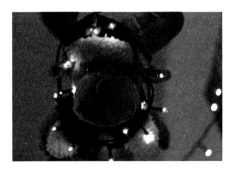

Rudolph's Claim to Fame

With all the talk about Rudolph and reindeer games this time of year, it's time to set the story straight on a few matters. What's the difference between a reindeer and a deer? Why is Rudolph the popular one? I mean, sure he has a shiny nose, but still …

As for the first question, all reindeer are deer, but not all deer are reindeer (even though they are all dear). Reindeer are specific to cold regions like, well, the North Pole. They are actually considered caribou and have hoofs that allow them to walk (perhaps fly?) in snowy climates. Reindeer are a bit bigger than deer, and it's the only species of deer where the females grow antlers. (Vixen does sport some pretty lovely ones.)

And as for Rudolph, the red-nosed reindeer was the brilliant creation of one Mr. Robert May back in 1939. He wrote a book featuring Rudolph for Montgomery Ward as an economically-efficient giveaway to customers. Ten years later, Robert's brother-in-law set it to music and created a catchy tune that Gene Autry recorded. And the rest is history.

Seasonal Side note: On the evening of December 6, 1964, families sat down to watch a new TV show for the first time: an animated special called Rudolph the Red-Nosed Reindeer. It featured the voice of Burl Ives as Sam, a singing snowman who narrates the tale of a misfit reindeer who finds his own special way to

shine. The hour-long show went on to become not only the longest-running and highest-rated Christmas special in TV history, but also a beloved holiday tradition."

~ *United States Postal Service 2015*

The Twelve Days of Christmas

If you've heard the Christmas carol "… and a partridge in a pear tree," then you might be wondering what's with twelve days of Christmas and all of those presents? Many think it is the twelve days leading up to the 25th of December, but actually, those twelve days start the day after our celebrated December 25th.

 This is the reason why some take down holiday decorations only after the 6th of January. Both the carol and the "twelve-day" concept are more than likely based on religious beliefs leading right up to the eve of the Epiphany, the climax of the Advent/Christmas Season.

The Epiphany represents the day that the three kings arrived in Bethlehem with gifts of (you guessed it) gold, frankincense, and myrrh. You've got the gold part. Frankincense and myrrh are both derived from tree bark and are fragrant essential oils. There are various interpretations about the meaning of these gifts and what they represent, both as medicinal herbs and as symbolic statements. Let's just say it took a while to follow that North star (twelve days to be precise), to bestow the precious presents. No Amazon Prime in those days.

As for the colorful "red-legged" partridge, the star of the carol is commonly found in France, so if the song drives you a little crazy, you can probably blame it on the French.

It's a Snowman Kind of Sing

Snowmen are a big thing this time of year. The nice ice structure takes the lead in plenty of Christmas carols, that have us pining for wintry snow days where we can go walking in a winter wonderland and build a snowman in the meadow, pretending that he's Parson Brown.

Wait, what's a parson? The carol "Winter Wonderland" was written back in the 1930s when words like vicar, rector, or parson referred to men of the cloth or clergy. Today, we're more inclined to use minister or priest. In the tune, the lovebirds out walking want to play wedding and get hitched, so a snowman will do.

Then there's our old pal, Frosty, who just wants to come out and play before he melts away. But isn't it interesting that there's not one word of Christmas mentioned in the entire original "Frosty the Snowman" song? Go ahead, sing it. I'll wait.

With the success of Rudolph the Red-nosed Reindeer, Gene Autry was asked once again to sing this new 1950s tune in hopes of another hit. It worked. So much so, that a made-for-TV cartoon special was created for the holidays. It was then that the very last line of the song that Frosty sings was changed  to "I'll be back on Christmas Day!" making him, and snow people everywhere, forever a Christmas staple. It's good to be a snowman.

12

Last-Minute Gifts

"Hurray! Santa is packing his sleigh, and the elves are busy charting the route for tomorrow night's big fly!" You hear those cries of delight from the children and find yourself thinking, "Yipes! Christmas Eve is tomorrow? How did that happen?"

Invariably, the holiday sneaks upon us, leaving too little time to get everything done. At some point, you just have to call it a holiday and sit back to enjoy time with loved ones, which is the real spirit of the season. But for those of you who still clamor for last-minute treasures or just found out about unexpected guests you need a gift for, there are still options.

- **Local drugstore.** You'll be amazed at what you can find here! Smaller crowds, great deals on a wide range of goodies along with all the holiday essentials, plus staples like a gallon of milk or pet food. When push comes to shove, the drugstore is always your best friend for last-minute items.

- **Grocery store.** You can usually find gift cards near the check-out aisle. Some say that gift cards aren't personal or that not enough thought goes into it, but I disagree. If any gift says "hey, I was thinking about you and wanted to get you a little something," it's a gift card. Try to choose a gift card that makes sense for the recipient and add a note for a personal touch.

- **Floral shop.** Go in, pick your own loose flowers (they'll usually arrange them for you), and you're done! A beautiful, fresh small bouquet is a wonderful sentiment without delivery frustration.

- **Garden home centers, hardware stores, and big box stores**. Grab a small potted plant or herb, a garden tool, or any of the holiday items they have on sale. Whether it's firewood for the chimney or cinnamon pine cones in a bag, there are always good finds and good discounts.

- **Neighborhood bakery**. Grab some sweets or fresh bread and add a bow. No one denies the love of sweet treats.

- **Gas station.** Purchase gas gift cards while you are filling up. Who couldn't use a little gas these days?

Seasonal Tip: If you do find yourself at the mall during the hectic busy time, rest up next to Santa's chair and watch the kids as they bounce excitedly into his lap. Gaze at the holiday decorations and pick up some of that festive energy to carry you through.

Gifts from Home and the Heart

If you're all out of cash and can't bear to make another trip to any location, you can find everything you need right at home.

- Copy down a few of your best recipes (or borrow some from Mom or the web) and bundle the cards as a great gift. Better yet, package up some homemade treats.

- Print a photo and display it in a home-made frame. It could be a family photo, a picture of a flower, a great vacation destination, or anything that the person might enjoy. Place the photo on a sheet of paper, and enlist the kids to design a frame with crayons or colored pens, or do the honors yourself.

- Take a trip into your own backyard and employ the kids again or DIY to make a great arrangement with your own greenery.

- Make coupons for deeds that make the recipient's life a little easier, such as dog-walking, shoveling snow, or babysitting.

- Build a music playlist or create a photo CD (or enlist your technically savvy kids to lend you a hand).

- Give one of those books sitting on the shelf a new home. If you enjoyed reading it, your friend might, too. It isn't doing much gathering dust, and you can always replace it later if you must own a copy.

Go on, get creative! There are so many items around the house that lend to great gift giving. It's a wonderful gesture, and small tokens of friendship are usually the best gift of all.

13

CHAPTER THIRTEEN

Beating the Christmas Blues

A Christmas Memory

In the 1970s, little Meg asked her parents hundreds of times if she could get a TV of her very own for Christmas. The answer was always the same: no. One year, much to Mom's chagrin, Dad gave in on his way home from work on Christmas Eve and bought a small television. Of course, Meg was thrilled Christmas morning with this special gift that gave her hours of enjoyment, and she hung on to it through the years.

Eventually, little Meg grew up and the TV went into the attic to gather dust. One Christmas, she was particularly feeling the pain of losing her father and missing him terribly. Then, she recalled the childhood set, which had been replaced by a state-of-the-art

screen long ago. The dusty set was cleaned up and placed under the tree. Meg still felt the warmth and glow of that holiday magic her dad had given her so many years before.

Ghosts of Christmas Past

It's no surprise there are people who have a very difficult time with emotions during the holidays. We may struggle with challenging relationships beyond just horrible in-laws or bad sweater gifts. Christmas can augment emotional pain as we reflect on our past. We long for change in the connections with the people in our lives, needing some to be closer and others to have more distance. That's the time to cherish good memories and forge ahead to new beginnings. Each Christmas brings us an opportunity to forgive and to be forgiven.

Sometimes the holidays are a sad reminder of the ones who are no longer with us, and it can be much to bear. This is all the more reason to express the season in your own way and make the holiday yours. Be kind to yourself. Honor those you love by engaging in Christmas magic. Look for ways to enjoy a part of the holiday that you know they loved. Know their spirit lives on within you and share the joy. It's a time of reflection and renewal. Make it meaningful in your heart. After all, there's no better season for small miracles, bringing tidings of great comfort and joy.

'Twas the night AFTER Christmas, and all through the house …

… there were opened presents and wrapping paper strewn about and leftovers galore. Ah, December 26th. Gifts lie askew, wrapping paper ripped and scattered, new toys buzzing and chugging away, all the celebration and excitement still smoldering like the fire in the hearth. Hopefully, you're relaxing in your new robe and fuzzy slippers, basking in the afterglow of Christmas cheer with enough stored in your heart, and extra, to fill up the memory basket.

After all our complaints of Christmas coming too fast, inevitably it is gone too soon. The melancholy aftermath of emotions begins to settle in as we prepare to de-Christmatize (my word for packing it all away—works, doesn't it?). Time to store the tree decorations and sweep up the season's glitter. Don't want it to end? Don't forget, the twelve days of Christmas begin on the 26th and take you right through New Year celebrations and beyond. You can gently slide into a new, fresh year, your way.

The Keepsake Letter

But hold on! Before you finally muster up the energy to take down the ornaments and call it a Christmas, sit down next to your Christmas tree with a cup of cheer. Take out a sheet of paper and write a letter to yourself. Go ahead. It's only to you, and it's a safe place where you can write down all your wishes for the new year, and reflect on the highlights and feelings of the past year soon to be ushered out. Give yourself words of encouragement, hope, forgiveness, prosperity, whatever you need or want.

Once you've written it all
down, seal it in an envelope
and put your name on it.
Place it in a decorative box
where the tree ornaments
will be stored. Next year,
long after you've forgotten
about it, you'll discover a
great reminder of all you've
accomplished along with
your most poignant thoughts last season. You'll realize you can
get through anything!

Get the whole clan involved in letter writing. It's a great tradition,
one that's sure to bring you a smile when you give yourself the
gift of very special memories.

Although the once-a-year day is behind you, steal a moment to
congratulate yourself on a Christmas well done. Hopefully this
one stands out as your best ever, because you really were in the
moment, enjoying all that is and continues to be meaningful
for you. Linger in the spirit, right through ringing in the new
year. Don't stop taking back your holidays now that you've got
the hang of it. And should you ever need a gentle reminder, Dr.
Xmas will be right here for you, with your prescription. Merry
Christmas! …and happy holidays.

About the Author

Meet Dr. Xmas, your consummate holiday expert. Born on December 25th (we'll save the year), the holiday has held a special place in her heart since she was a tiny tot. She's made Christmas and all its festivities, myths, and folklore her niche. Exploring Christmas, its joy and magic, and what it means to those around her, is where she puts just some of her unstoppable, bubbly yuletide energy.

Dr. Xmas has a life-long connection to Christmas as well as a passion for education and literature. She's a UCLA graduate in Linguistics and English and earned a Master's degree in English Education from Syracuse University. She is an educator, a writer, and a business woman. In her spare time, she dabbles in a full-time career in media marketing.

She's a champion for taking back our holidays, leading the charge to make them less stressful and more enjoyable. Her goal? To spread good tidings of great cheer and all things Tiny Tim to a sometimes too-busy-

for-Christmas world. Whew! Now that's something worth striving for, don't you think?

Yvonne Lacey, affectionately known as Dr. Xmas, lives in Los Angeles, California. She's a beach junky who lives for Christmas, good cheer, and sand between her toes.

Now, Take Back Your Holidays

How will you take back your holidays this year?

Use the following pages to jot down your own ideas, plans, Christmas wishes, doodles, recipes, or memories. It's up to you!

Visit www.Drxmas.com for holiday inspiration all year long and to share your holiday tips and magic.

_____

_____

_____

_____

_____

_____

_____

_____

_____

_____

_____

Made in the USA
San Bernardino, CA
27 October 2017